A MEAL LIKE THAT

A MEAL LIKE THAT

Poems by Albert Garcia

BRICK ROAD
POETRY PRESS

Also by Albert Garcia

Skunk Talk (Bear Star Press, 2005)
Digging In: Literature for Developing Writers (Prentice Hall, 2004)
Rainshadow (Copper Beech Press, 1996)

Cover credit: Terence R. Duren
                  Picnic in the Park, oil on canvas, c. 1944
                  Gift of Eloise (Dierks) Andrews Kruger and Miller &
                      Paine/R.E. Campbell Collection, Museum of
                      Nebraska Art Collection

Author photo: Teresa Steinbach-Garcia

Library of Congress Control Number: 2015939867
ISBN-13: 978-0-9898724-5-4

Published by Brick Road Poetry Press
P. O. Box 751
Columbus, GA 31902-0751
www.brickroadpoetrypress.com

Brick Road logo by Dwight New

Across the street the old man signals
from his garden. With two hands
he is holding up a big tomato for you to see.

For Carl, Doris, Ascencion, and Josefina—
and all the rest

What is all this juice and all this joy?

—Gerard Manley Hopkins

Acknowledgments

Grateful acknowledgement is made to the following journals, in which these poems (sometimes in earlier versions) first appeared:

Bellingham Review: "Tomatoes on Interstate 5"
Concho River Review: "Hit by Pitch"
Cloudbank 6: "Into the Sun," "Trash Fish"
Cutthroat: "Beyond," "Boy Cleaning Trout," "Ritual"
Fugue: "River Scent"
Hawaii Pacific Review: "Mosquitofish"
Naugatuck River Review: "November Task"
New Plains Review: "Cussing in the 4th Grade"
The North American Review: "The Sea of Galilee and the Sacramento River"
Poems and Plays: "Elephant Heart," "Home from Work," "The Weather and Your Dress"
Willow Springs: "Dig"

"Boy Cleaning Trout" also appeared in *New California Writing 2011* from Heyday, edited by Gayle Wattawa.

Contents

Five

Six

Mosquitofish

The mosquitofish in the pond
wait for the insect to lay its eggs,
for the wriggling larvae to hatch.

Then they swim over, slurp up
their little meal and retreat
to the lily pads' shelter

having saved me from the irritating welts
of early summer. Wouldn't it be great
if we could all gorge ourselves

to protect each other? I'd take on
a sixteen ounce porterhouse and a bottle
of Syrah to keep my mother

from the chronic ache in her joints.
Would a meal like that
save my friend from the dark

pain of his marriage
ending—or salve my wife's
migraines with cool relief?

Give me a wide wedge of that banana
cream pie so I can shelter you,
my friendly reader, from the diseased hours

of your day. Let us sit
at the table, reach across each other
for extra helpings of potatoes and gravy.

Of course, the mosquitofish
know not what they do. They eat
to fill their one-inch silver bellies,

oblivious to good or harm. Perhaps
it's better that way, to rescue
by accident, swimming through algae

each day of your life, never knowing you stop
the rash before it starts. Just think,
as you slather butter on bread,

tearing at the crusty heel of sourdough
with your teeth, how good you are.
You could be saving us now.

One

Advent

Before the gifts and wrappings, before
tins of shortbread my grandmother sent
every year, before Confession, before Mass, before I knew
what I didn't want to know, I'd lie
beneath the tree, near the heater vent,
listening to the rumble of warmth
beneath the house, smelling the carpet,
the pine-fresh basin of water
in the stand. Of course I'd dream
of impossible gifts: fishing rods, guns
I was too young for, elaborate electric football
games where the plastic players sprinted
down the sideline on a cushion of air.
My dreams were simple: catch a long bomb
from John Brodie, catch a big trout.
This was before I knew love is pain
wrapped in shining paper, that the dream
itself is the gift. I would lie
under that silver tip, picking off short needles,
pinching them to smell
what was right on hand, what I already knew
was a season of hope, what I'd carry with me
into the world of Santa and Jesus.

Boy Cleaning Trout

His father taught him
the belly, the only white part,
should give with the tip of his knife,
so he keeps pushing until its soft flesh splits
and the blade slides easily
up between fins to the head.

Just down riffle, his father watches
the boy spreading it open. The meat
should be his first concern: orange-red
it's native, white
it's fed in a hatchery—no taste.
He looks for its sex,
a pearly skein of roe the color of cantaloupe
or a thin thread of sperm
tucked back against its spine.

He works his fingers
under the cool entrails, pulls hard,
tosses all but the white tube,
the gut, into the stream. This
he squeezes between finger and thumb
to see a gray mash,
the fish's last meal of mayflies.

His knuckles white-red with cold, he rubs

the cavity thoroughly, rinses, then hooks

the burgundy feathers hidden

under shining flaps of its head.

His father taught him long ago

that these take oxygen from water,

that all living things need oxygen.

He notices the little cloud escaping his lips

and remembers the fish's mouth

opening and opening, gills

lifting in what looked like exhaustion

but could have been pain.

First Communion, 1970

The first time I hold my tongue out
for the priest, I fear
his white fingers will touch
my mouth above the gold plate
in the alter boy's hesitant hand.

There I kneel at the oak rail,
staring at the statue of Jesus,
his red, revealed heart,
a plum circled with thorns.
I feel the gaze of St. Patrick
peering down from the stained glass,
serpent pinned beneath his feet.

I feel Sister Mary Raymond's hope
I'll become a priest,
she who gave our catechism class
keychain medals of Neil Armstrong's
"one small step" and warned us
never to forget this miracle,
this act of God. I swallow—

the scratchy host
nearly catching in my throat—
return to the cool comfort
of my pew. Saints and angels look down
from the ceiling, down
upon my slicked hair.

I am seven years old. My new
Rosary beads shine black,
a clutch of ripe elderberries
in my small hands.

On the church's front steps after Mass,
I join my class for a photo,
starched white shirts and ruffled dresses,
black ties and tulle veils—
everyone squinting into the blaze
of spring sun that hangs over Main Street.

I'm the one in the middle
with the worried smile,
asking myself how the Lord decides
who raises lunar dust
with his steps, who stands
behind the altar in flowing vestments.

Awkward in my nicest clothes, I struggle

to look at the camera, to focus,

wondering if God, resting in my stomach

even now, knows who I am.

Lent

To be like Jesus, I gave up
lemon drops and black licorice,
which I didn't like anyway.

It wasn't exactly wandering
forty days in the desert,
but it was sacrifice

since I would have used both
to barter with friends
for cat eye marbles or baseball cards.

Oh, I knew what was coming.
Every year a man suffered
on a cross, was given vinegar

to drink, was mocked by a crowd
while his friends shrunk away
in fear or shame. Every year

I prepared for this
by giving something up
and confessing to the priest

that I'd taken the Lord's name
in vain, had been mean
to my sisters, had disobeyed

my parents. These sins earned me
ten Our Fathers of penance,
prayers to be said immediately,

kneeling in the dark cavern of the church,
staring at the statue of Jesus
hanging sinewy on the cross.

That's where I saw him
every Sunday, suspended
in front of the congregation,

watching me fidget in the pew,
knowing my every impure thought
while I stared at the stained-glass

saints in the windows. They stared
back with Jesus like teachers
waiting for me to turn in a test.

I searched my soul, or tried,
not knowing exactly where to find it,
worried it had already slipped away

and gone outside where the spring air
was hot and light, where you could taste
pleasure on the breeze.

Cussing in the 4th Grade

As we expected, it made us more mature.
We roamed the playground, impressing all
who would listen with our *hells*
and *goddamits,* our suddenly sage
observations made emphatic by impeccable
adult diction we'd learned from older brothers.
When my buddy, Pat, saw a skinny kid
fall from the monkey bars, he said, poetically,
Bitchin' dismount. I was a novice
but still able to praise my friend's killer
jumpshot. *Damn,* I said, and again, *Damn.*
We learned syntax and rhythm. We learned
to push out our chests and wave our arms
in important gestures. Nothing could stop
our wit and charm as we egged each other on,
ignoring Sister Carolita's stern warnings
not to take the Lord's name in vain. Sure,
I got smacked by my mom; the principal
paddled Pat 'til he swore he'd never
swear again. But we were now part
of another order, those who knew
the dirty alley and back door of our language,
who could praise, who could cut, who could sing
down the halls, across the blacktop, beyond.

Two

Free Throws

Fluid off the fingertips,
arced though fifteen feet of air—you hear
a silk swish, leather and twine.

Unguarded, you're supposed to make these
with involuntary ease. Your body,
on its own, will know the motion.

Early in your marriage,
you made thirty-seven straight in your driveway,
the only witness your infant daughter,

watching in her wind-up swing, your wife
on evening shift at the fabric store. When you missed
on thirty-eight, you stopped, looked around to imprint

the event in your mind—there in the dusk, there
in the floodlight's shadows—
and hoped that impossible streak

meant something. It didn't.
Or if it did you never recognized it,
even though you remember still the perfect

repetition of your shot, the way
you held it together despite the night's
quiet pressure, your pulse, the rhythmic

squeak of your daughter's swing. There you were
dreaming yourself on arena hardwood,
ready to box out a six-eight power forward

until you lifted your daughter
and kissed her. *You see that?* you asked, and soon
it was history, story, nothing more

than what you could prove to nobody,
thirty-seven free throws, an act of brilliance
no one would notice or believe,

foul shots without the foul, a gift you gave
yourself one fall evening, a feat you knew
at once you would never live again.

Cleanse

Before moving in, we scrubbed the cupboards
inside and out. We painted,

carpeted, sucked the heating ducts
of their dust and smoke.

We tore curtains from their rods,
left them draped from the garbage bin

by the road. Still, after a trip
to the ocean, a week of seaside walks

and wind in our hair, we open
the front door and it's there,

like sickness, infection,
the sour-pallid smell

we scoured from the bathroom tile.
The entryway walls

breathe the stain of those lives
we'd tried to strip with the wallpaper.

Dual panes closed for years to the south breeze,
whatever dreams this family had

were deep-plowed into the field,
left to be overrun by tarweed and mullein.

If we were to live in this house, we knew
we must take what seeped from the attic

and under floorboards, from dank corners
of closets and cabinets,

and replace that air with our own
breath, a little tired but still alive,

what we used to make the rafters lift
the heavy burden of the past.

Beyond

Its body like onion skin, a dead dragonfly,
moved by the breeze, scratches
along the concrete in front of my garage.
No longer does it hover at the pond
where, just the other day, I saw two
connected in midair, an iridescent
mating in the breeze. It's no longer on the tip
of the sedge jutting from the mud.
My cat sees me bend to touch it,
bats it gently breaking off one wing.
I pick up that wing, place it in my palm,
drag it along the back of my hand,
a wing that is lighter than anything
I'll ever feel, a wing that when held
to the sky is like the lace
my grandmother put over her guest room
window, which veiled a view
of a field and mountains beyond.

A Short Essay on What Is Nice

That young woman in the market
looks nice. Her white blouse,
neatly pressed, looks nice. White linen
is nice. The word *blouse* is nice.
So is the word *sundress,*
a nice bit of associated clothing
one could imagine on this young woman
in a park, at a picnic. The way
she reached out and grabbed
a mango and brought it to her face
to smell was nice. Likewise,
her manner of placing the fruit
gently in her basket. Likewise,
the way she carried that basket
to the display of baguettes,
as if acting in a film
as if knowing someone might have noticed.

Twig by Twig

Bothered by something, he followed a trail
through mint and ferns down to the creek
where he paused by a pool, took a breath,
and waded in to lie on the bottom,
back pressed into the silty gravel.
Opening his eyes to peer up
through the current into the sky,
he stayed in the cold until holding
his breath became easy, until the water
seemed to slow and the surface
grew still—and he could see clearly
the overhanging alder, its trembling leaves,
a kingfisher perched with crested head,
its dripping black beak, minnow writhing.

Hit by Pitch

Everybody knows he won't rub it.
He drops his bat, winces,
carries the fastball's searing pain
to first. The crowd heard
a thud, then their own
collective moan like the murmur
of pigeons. He's heard
the whistling freight of the ball,
an inexplicable ringing
in his head, his spikes crunching
the cindery dirt as he walks
that ninety feet of chalk he's earned.

After he takes his three-step lead,
after the first baseman jokes,
Yeah, he hangs that curve
now and then, after he misses
the coach's sign, he lifts
his chest in breath that aches
his lungs open with cool air.
It's enough to get him through
the next pitch, through the pop fly
to short that gets him into the dugout,
into the evening at home

where he sees in the bathroom mirror

the yellow-green reminder

in his white flesh, just above

his hip, a faint pattern of Vs

left by the stitching, those red threads

he still hears spinning right in front of him.

Raspberries

He plops them in the green mesh basket,
knowing they are through
feeding each other, knowing he can pull
until the vine rips but only ripe
berries will give with a gentle tug
releasing themselves to the faint
pressure of his skin.

Picking in morning-cool sun,
he thinks of placing them
on her tongue,
between her lips of nearly the same
color. So delicate the movement,
from afar one might assume
he is soothing some small wound.

Three

The Sea of Galilee and the Sacramento River

I figured they were steelhead, those fish

that tore the nets and filled two boats

after Jesus told Simon Peter to cast

into deeper water. Ten years old, fidgeting

in my family's pew, in the dark light

of Sacred Heart Catholic Church,

I could only imagine Jesus and Simon

wearing hip waders, standing in an autumn riffle

of the Sacramento, pulling in one

shining sea-run rainbow after another.

Simon starts to believe after Jesus

shows him the right size fly and how

to present it. And when Monsignor Casey

read Simon's repentant plea—

"Depart from me, Lord, for I am a sinful man"—

I thought, too bad, and dwelled

on nets ripping, flapping silver filling

the boats, joyful shouts of fishermen

lining the banks. I just knew

how Simon and the others had felt that day,

how a guy can spend hour after hour

staring into dark currents,

waiting for a sign or someone to lead him

upstream to better water, only to trudge

back home with an empty ice chest.

So when Monsignor read that they dropped everything

and followed, my mind gleamed

with the scales of a thousand fish

and I thought, yeah, I'd tag along with that guy, too.

Elephant Heart

Named for its size and the purple-red
meat of its flesh, this plum comes ripe
in late summer, fruit bending the branches
to the ground. This is a plum
a boy likes to pick and hold in his hand,
a firm plum lobbed above his head
and caught, an easy pop-fly, a plum
he can't resist heaving through the sticky air
of singing gnats toward the pickup,
the dusty windshield's glare.
Imagine the thump, the spatter,
the satisfying arc onto the road.

But in this story of desire,
the plum misses, driver unaware,
fruit landing inaudibly in the hot grass
of the ditch across the road.
The boy looks back at the farmhouse
he grew up in. No one has seen him.
Two wild turkeys scratch around
the flower beds, ruffling feathers
off their bodies in the heat.
The boy cups his fingers and palm
around another plum, twists it

until it releases from the branch.

He cocks his arm back.

He hears another car.

Creeks

Walk in and feel the stones,
round and slimed with moss,
in the arches of your feet. Feel the warm

water of the shallows, tadpoles darting off,
fingerling bluegill
easing into shadows. You're six. Your mother

brought you to this summer creek
to swim, to learn the pleasure
of getting cool in the sultry heat

of this valley. How could you see
across the levee, on the other side
of the world, men slogged up another creek

in a place called the Mekong Delta,
packs slung over their backs, rifles
raised above their helmets? How could you know

why they were there
or if they knew? You'd learn later
many never made it

and many returned haunted

by the water. Here you were, a kid

whose skinny legs poked down

like an egret's, caught up in a world of water striders,

those creatures that can stay afloat

by surface tension,

and the pollywogs using their wide tails

and undeveloped legs

to push their fleshy bodies to safety.

Trash Fish

Sucker, Sacramento squawfish, carp:
we cursed if we hooked up,
thrashed our poles in air
to jostle them off the lure.
We didn't want to touch
these water vermin, the dull brown slime
of their scales. Casting for trout—
firm silver sides and blue backs—
we knew these others cruised
the bottom, sucking what nutrients
they could from the slime.
We'd toss them onto the bank,
round stones crusted with algae,
and watch their pathetic mouths
open and open.
                    Imagine us,
two boys on the bend of a river,
under autumn sky so crisp
you could see from a mile downstream
the steeple of our church and the spire
of Zuckweiler's Department Store
on Main Street, where every April
the rodeo parade marched along
with high school bands, prancing

Arabians, last year's county queen—
so much flashy paint and chrome
in the fire engine's gleam.
Lining the street, hunkered down
on the curb, we watched, amazed, dull eyes
peering from our mottled skin,
our odd misshapen faces.

Pistol

In his parent's bedroom closet, on the shelf
above his father's pressed white shirts
and next to his mother's hatbox,

the boy finds the .38. He stands
tiptoe, grabs the cold crosshatched butt
with his fingers, sits on the carpet,

and admires it as a thing to hold,
an object with weight
and scent—the cologne of gun oil

he's smelled on his father's return
from cutting firewood. That was when
his dad carried it, protection against rattlers

he couldn't hear over the roar
of the chainsaw. The boy slips
the gun in and out of its leather holster.

He releases the magazine, empty
as he knew it would be, and pops it
back with the heel of his hand,

a move that says he's in control
of something important. Taking aim
on the bedside lamp, he lifts the pistol

with both hands, working the far-sight crest
into the near-sight notch, and squeezes,
imagining the kick, the bounce-back

of the muzzle, heat
in his palms. He runs his fingers
along the cool barrel, feels its smoothness,

its rugged hardness. In truth, he knows
his aim is poor. It's heavy, this gun, too much
to steady with his skinny outstretched arms

now lifting it back to the closet
shelf, as if never touched, as if what he feels
had not yet made him sweat.

Dig

The day my father's shovel bit

into something hard

and brought up fragments—

abalone shell

this far from the ocean!—

when he pulled out the trunk and roots

of the fruitless mulberry he'd felled

and revealed in the hole

what they'd been cradling—

a skeleton, a child's,

an Indian's—I stared

at the bones, the black dirt,

the small round pieces of shell

and knew I should be quiet.

I decided she was a girl,

her skull small, eye sockets

looking up from where she lay

half embedded in soil, half

once again in the valley's

winter air. I wasn't old enough

to see this land without an orchard,

a grassy alluvial plain stretching down

to the river, but I could imagine her

picking blackberries with her mother
along the creek behind our property,
filling baskets. Her small fingers,
not so different from mine,
grew stained with the berries' juice.

My father tried a few stories: maybe
she caught a disease, was killed
by a mountain lion or bear,
or drowned in the river.
Can I touch?
I was ten. I wanted those bones
and, kneeling, leaned into the shallow grave,
felt blood rush to my face.

Nearly upside-down,
I ran my finger along
the edge of her pelvis
jutting through the soil like a bowl
until my father started shoveling,
filling the grave
and I was on my feet again, my head
dizzy, hands on my own skinny hips,
and listened to the hole receive
soft thuds of dirt, the rhythm
of my father's work, the sounds
of a straining body, of breathing.

Four

Tomatoes on Interstate 5

Trucks roll down I-5, trailers full
of tomatoes. Almost always
they'll spill a few as they round a corner,

hard, small fruit
bouncing over asphalt,
a bright scattering of red

on the road's shoulder
of star thistle and tarweed.
Maybe you left the house

angry over an argument with your wife,
words in the air
like a whining fan belt. Maybe

you're headed down the freeway
because it's the fastest way out
of town and you're suddenly sick

of the same streets and just have to drive
to something new. You're in your car,
mind dulled by the flatness of rice fields,

their green monotony, when somewhere
in your vision's periphery a pheasant
coasts over the road

almost hitting the big rig in front of you.
The trucker taps his breaks
and it happens: spilling, filling your view,

tomatoes bouncing around your car
in a flash of color so sudden
you wonder if this is real

or if it's something else that's made
your pulse quicken, your grip
tighten on the wheel. In the rearview

you see them roll onto the shoulder's
hot gravel, and you can't help it—
you keep glancing in the mirror,

feeling lucky, wanting to say something
though no one is sitting
beside you, and you drive

until the small red dots are gone

and the road bends

into the dreary gray grove of olives.

Home from Work

What to do? I'll eat a few cubes
of watermelon diced and chilled
in the fridge. Then I'll pat the hound
on his head and let him lick
the juice from my fingers. After that
I'll read the headlines—all I can stand—
or just the ads in the sports section.
I'll talk to the dog. I'll tell him
about the meeting where everyone fought
over the agenda. He'll breathe
his heavy dog breath of impatience.
He'll tell me someone needs to get the axe.
He'll say gimme a bite of that melon.
He'll say maybe it should be you.

Presentation

The way you laughed at the meeting
sounded like an animal dying,

halting, uneasy, so I didn't believe
your nervous proposal or that you

could lead anything requiring people
to follow you. Your eyes

like small flakes of bronze said something
entirely other than what you wanted.

You wanted me to join you. You wanted me
to say yes to whatever it was

you were pitching, but I could see
only that your smile, large and open-

mouthed, didn't match the sound
of the words leaving your lips,

words that quickly filled all corners
of the room like small birds flying up

against each other, so much movement,
so much energy in their chaotic flapping

that I wanted to run, wanted to dash out
into the courtyard where language

resided in things: bricks, fountain—a pigeon
sitting composed on the building's ledge.

Early Morning, Studying Art

Back from the Art Institute, my wife has taped
postcards to the freezer door.

I spot them in the morning
when I'm making coffee, the images

of two forlorn women: Max Klinger's
"Abandoned," sepia etching of a figure

who walks a beach with her head bowed,
face in her hands, the hem of her long dress

dragged in the wet sand—
and Munch's "Girl in the Window,"

who stands in a nighttime frame of light
offered by a streetlamp. She wears

a housedress or a nightgown—hard to tell—
and seems to be reading, holding

the book close to her face in dim light. I hold
the postcards in the morning cold

of our kitchen, wondering, why these?
Did she want me to see her

through the impossibly distant
stories of these lives? Was she saying,

Look, that's me, that's the way
I feel? In Klinger's fine lines

the woman seems ready to melt in the air
or water. Where is she going,

wandering the shore's edge, so lost
in the kind of emptiness

we all brace ourselves against?
Who abandoned her? Does it matter?

Does art require empathy? My wife
sleeps upstairs in a room still dark

in winter morning, a room that could be
painted in stark hues of another century.

How would Mr. Munch paint her
as she rises from sleep, still

sitting on the bed, her eyes
not yet part of this world,

not reading, not yet trying
to forget whatever small thing

will put the day's first expression
on her vacant, mysterious face?

Night Visit

That morning in the cabin I woke
with two small seeds
of mouse dung on my pillow,
black against the white cotton.

I hadn't dreamed, hadn't heard
the small feet, the thin bare tail
sliding over fabric.
Had he stopped—for how long—
to peer into my face? Maybe
he sat, soaking up
the waves of my warm breath
steady and gentle. That small brain—
had it registered a thought,
something basic about the pillow's
stuffing—nest material?
Maybe he just rested, rolling
a bit of food in his jowls.

I like to think, in the cold of my room,
he saw my eyes
dart beneath their lids, something
that would make him flinch
or run. It's nice to imagine

his pointed gray face

staring in curiosity or sympathy or hate.

What could he know of my dreams?

What could I know of his?

What I Wanted to Say

What I wanted to say,
the words to convince you,
flew away like my notes
from the patio table, a strong breeze
scraping them across the paver stones
and into the pond.

Okay, whether I was right or wrong,
I was wrong. Your tears said it,
the Virginia creeper draping the fence
between the front and back yards
said it, the way you held your hands
together in your lap said it.

At a certain point, I stopped talking,
swallowed every syllable.
Your eyes focused past my shoulder
and watched this evening's ordinary sun
walking its way
over the edge of the world.

Everything in my history
decomposed, compost heaped
in a pile, heating itself from within.

I offered up all my thoughtful gestures

like bouquets of daylilies.

They dripped clear sap from their stems.

Park Bench

There should be a park bench.
We'll sit next to each other,

watching a man throw a tennis ball
to his yellow lab, sending

and retrieving the dog
whose loyalty to task is clear

to both of them. I'll say something
to start, something I've wanted

to say for years, words I've never before
been able to put together,

and you'll hear them perfectly,
my words like a child's wooden blocks

you can hold in your hands,
turning them for their modest gleam.

What you say comes as a breeze
that sinks in my skin,

not warm, not cool, just
what I needed to feel and hear,

like bath water, like tea. Then
we sit, and the dog

lopes out again to retrieve
his ball. The man waits

for what he knows is coming,
and the breeze, if there,

moves between us, back
and forth, silently.

Current

Across the valley, past melon farms
and laser-leveled rice fields
the river bends south

through a band of green—sycamore,
cottonwood, vines of wild grape,
scrubby patches of blackberry and poison oak

holding to the levee. This time of year
American shad—strong, bony fish—
swim upstream from the ocean.

Catch one and it will slap
dime-sized scales on the rocks.
You could come for a picnic

but you stop here when your husband talks
too much about the woman sales rep
from Fresno. You need

to step in and feel the numb
rise up your legs. You need
any story that is not your own.

But they're all yours now,
a whole riverbed of lives
stretching miles to the delta.

Just last month divers yanked out
the bloated body of a kid who fished
and drank all night

until the river made him disappear.
They dislodged his pale flesh
from a snag two miles down

from where he parked his truck.
You wonder if he wanted to die,
if the intoxicating smell of green

water in moonlight just took him in.
You wonder if he'd caught any fish,
if he'd felt quick taps,

long pulls, the tug tug tug
in his hands. You wonder
if the heron on the far bank

saw anything. There he is,
wading, motionless for minutes
while you hear your heart

in your chest until he spears
the surface with his head,
quick flash above the shine

of current. That same cold current
makes the bones in your feet ache.
All you want to do

is forget, but the water insists
you feel it in your flesh
before it flows off around the bend

and toward the city of thousands
who come to the river's edge
to touch it.

Five

The Weather and Your Dress

Ah, when she moved, she moved in more ways than one . . .

—Theodore Roethke

The liquid angles of your dress
here at your breasts, here again

flowing over your hips,
pour themselves across my mind.

Mild February air has just begun
to stir, but we know Pacific fronts

swoop down off Alaska with winter's
numbing anger. Soon eucalyptus will dance

in the wind, a frenetic release
of leaves and twigs. For now

the hem over your knee moves
just a little, the cotton at your side

pressed lightly against you.
Yes, this has been a year of storms.

Each week we imagine
the weather map's new story—

hot and cold air masses that collide
in our skies. Each week

we brace ourselves
with thick sweaters and parkas.

But this minute, I swear, you spun
to look my way, and your dress

moved so I felt it
across the room, the very start of a breeze,

a new weather system from a land of warmth
and all that sways gently in the air.

Young Couple at Mass

At Mass the just-married couple
hold hands in the pew. New to the parish,
they sit in front of an elderly pair,
soapy scent of a 40-year marriage,
and behind a family whose eight-year-old
leans under the seats to stare
at the many ankles and shoes.

They feel noticeable, awkward—
familiar amid the statue
of the Virgin and stations of the cross,
yet objects of the faithful eyes
around them. It's true. At the base
of her neck and just below the short sleeves
of her blouse, her skin
blooms tan and healthy. It's too much.
The mother of four three pews back
and across the aisle senses
something indecent in that sun-blonde hair
and the way their shoulders touch.

When they stand for Communion,
the young man places his hand
on the small of his wife's back

to usher her into the aisle.

Square shoulders and crewcut,

he walks in line just inches behind her.

Despite the choir, she hears him breathing.

Morning, Dillon Beach

The ocean's breath is cold
this morning. It smells old

and distant. Sand fleas
fogging up around my ankles

have been here forever.
They rise from the remains

of dead crab and kelp, broken shells
and beds of dull gray pebbles.

With the waves' gentle lap and curl,
you'd say optimism should rise

like the cry of a gull.
There are no gulls.

You walk a hundred yards ahead of me,
head down, searching, your posture

saying, I'm tired, leave me alone
with the fog so I can blend in

to the morning's gray. Over here
charred driftwood and bottles

mark where local kids drank and smoked
just to be with each other.

That fire was lit a week ago
or a month. Maybe the charred logs

really washed up in a storm.
You're still walking up the beach,

hands in your jacket pockets,
further away now, less distinct.

Somebody's dog lopes out to join you
as if he were yours.

Into the Sun

That morning after the storm,
I counted seven small moles

scattered across your back. Later,
when we stepped outside,

the sun's brightness after a night of rain
made us squint and laugh.

In light like this everything
reveals itself: a sparrow

pecking gravel in a small puddle,
tiny beads of water

on the flowering maple's leaves, the way
you rub your hands briskly together

to warm them. I caught myself
watching you, wanting to say,

Do that again. Move your hair back
from your eyes just so—one more time.

Even a small scrap of paper
fallen from one of the cars

and lying damp on the wet blacktop
flapped a little, claiming its role

in the morning's shine. And honestly,
I hardly recognized your voice

when you called to me
though I stared right at you

and into the sun.

Equilibrium

You're on a beach in Maui,
toes in those first few feet
of swirling surge
where the finest white sand
lifts off the bottom and settles
again and again so that this edge
of the world is a little cloudy
and it seems that everything
under your feet breathes.

With sun on your shoulders,
the waves' reflective lapping,
you think you might faint
or the world might turn upside down,
the warm Pacific falling
with a massive sucking sound
off its floor of coral
and into the afternoon air
already heavy
with a moist breeze.

You never know what might happen
when the sky is this bright,
your wife on her towel,

engrossed in a book, a cardinal

hopping in the hot sand behind her.

Just the idea of standing

on a volcano's shoulder, your body

between land, air, and water

makes you brace for balance

as if something out at sea had tipped

the ocean bottom, the cause

of waves beyond the reef,

the sand slide beneath your feet.

Rake

Listen to the sound
my rake makes, pulling grass clippings
into a pile, making things neat.
Don't you love the idea of lawns, billions
of tiny plants shaved by whirring blades
into flat inviting expanses greened up
by nitrogen and water? They're how we make
order in this country, small
front yard square or acres framed
around our great estates. It's a fine job,
some spending money, for a boy to mow
his neighbor's place. When I was a boy,
I dreamed of a lawn that stretched
to the sea. I could feel my bare toes
in the cool grass. Women wore sundresses
and strolled with sandals
dangling from their fingers—a party,
tables covered in white,
small sandwiches, men in sport jackets
gathered in the trees' shade—
all connected by the rich
green carpet that was everywhere.
Off in the distance, someone pushed
a mower in perfectly parallel rows,

so far away the guests could never hear

the motor, could barely smell

the fresh-cut fescue. I know now

that was I behind the mower.

Was I ever at the party? Had I ever joined

the children playing softball

and tag? Somehow I recall

the pleasure of pushing a croquet wicket

into the grass, the soil's

resistance and give.

But mostly I recall the sound

of the mower and when the mower was silent

the rake, the sweep and brush

of the grass, all evened out

and smelling nice—as it is now

in my back yard, ready for a party

should one be started

while I'm lost in my work.

Wolf and Lamb

Isaiah 11:6

And, by extension, the crocodile,

submerged in the muddy Mara River, shall wait

as the wildebeest swim leisurely

one bank to the other. The whole migrating herd

will pass, even calves struggling in the current.

Elsewhere in the world's placid sunshine,

the grizzly will snore next to a fawn,

the eagle keeping watch from an enormous blue sky

over the rabbit family, down below,

soaking in the warmth around their burrow.

The orca in the Strait of Juan de Fuca

shall cruise right through the school of salmon,

shall pass the half-grown seal pup. We will not fear

the polar bear, mountain lion, tiger shark.

We shall rest easily with the hyena nuzzling our fingers.

Dazed by peace, we will forget to ask how long

this can last, how long before those who film

the great migration at the Mara notice birds

screeching off a tree in alarm as one croc downstream
rolls in current, jaws clamped around something big and
flailing.

Six

Fat

When her meal came, she sliced a wedge of fat

from her prime rib and pushed it to her plate's rim

where it sat glistening and oily, soft

and translucent. I still remember how

she nudged it past her foil-wrapped potato,

out of the blood-juice pooled around the medium-

rare meat. *You're beautiful,* I said. She said,

You always say that—come up with something

better. The Syrah went well with thick slabs

of beef; our talk swirled around the candle

between us. As her eyes searched mine for what

she wanted, my eyes settled on the remains

of her cold meal: potato skin, two spears

of asparagus, and that strip of fat,

now white, now gelatinous, and always

something I, not she, would swallow.

November Task

The sun, that lurid persimmon
over the row of eucalyptus,
will leave in minutes

but by then its stain will set
behind your eyes. Quit crying.
You're not carrying the shovel

to the field, digging a hole
in the muck of winter. You're not
hoofing it back to the garage

to lift our cat's emaciated body,
a bag of bones and tumors
into your arms. I try not to look

at the slip of pink tongue
she hasn't the energy
to keep in her mouth. She drools,

can't stop her body from trembling
when I set her beside the hole
facing the sun. She's beyond

turning to look at me. And you
are in the house
not wanting to know

the shovel's weight above my head,
the sound it makes falling
through wet air,

the dull thump and then another
before I slide her body,
muscles twitching, off the wet grass.

It tumbles into the dirt
like a small sack of fruit.
The soil, moist and heavy, sticks

to the shovel as I fill in the hole.
Don't ask what I expected or why
I can't bear to see you.

Spring Insomnia

Go to sleep, you say.
I tell myself the same
but listen to early spring frogs

mating in the pond. First one yelps,
then another, then a chorus.
When they settle down,

sated, I like to believe,
the neighbor's cats howl
at each other over territory

or sex. It's 2:15. I've been awake
for an hour and know
the gentle hand of sleep is off

stroking someone else's forehead.
In a matter of seconds
I consider a memo at work,

a waitress who served me lunch
uptown, and a foul shot I missed
in a JV non-league game

30 years ago. *Settle down,*
I tell myself, *settle down,* but memories
flock in like hungry crows.

The night, I figure, still
has half its darkness.
The whole world

asleep and turning
its private dreams toward morning
breathes. I think I can hear

every insect hatching, every twig
in the maple by our window
scratching the siding

of our house, which holds me
like a box a kid uses to keep
a downy bird, confused, fallen

from its nest. I turn
the pillow to feel its cool underside.
Rest, I urge myself, *rest.*

Ritual

When you bent forward with the brush,
your hair plumed like ink from a squid.
Need I tell you I liked it, the way
it opened dark into our room,
a liquid flash in the window's light?

I lay in bed looking up from my book.
You were lost in ritual, the stern beauty
of being at task—as if peering
into a lake's deep pool, trying to see
something you dropped
beyond the lapping surface.

I didn't ask what agile thoughts
swam with you at day's end.
We shared the whisper your brush made,
moving through your hair, the rhythmic
pull and bounce. And before I closed my eyes,
you turned a bit and I saw
your neck—lovely, white, exposed.

Delivery

It's cut, the milk-blue
      cord, twisted
      tether draped between

a mother's flushed flesh,
      her infant's
      pasty newness.

6:12 a.m. The halls outside
      delivery
      echo

a few quiet footsteps—
      nurses
      making rounds.

Outside, dew
      glazes
      the lawn sweeping

to the parking lot.
      A Japanese maple
      drips

from new red leaves.

    How

    does the man

in recovery stop

    dreaming

    of his heart's valves

flapping

    open

    like tide-washed

sea anemones?

    Is it pain

    or relief

the infant feels

    opening

    her lungs

that very first time,

    the headlong rush

    of air?

⌘

River Scent

It's death you smell
down by the river, decay
of leaves and the mudflat's sedge,
rot of salmon carcass,
algae dried white over gravel.

You smell it from your car,
window open to the spring sun,
idling in traffic on the bridge.
It's only a trace
of what the canyon carries
but you realize that scent—
of mud and freshwater clam,
of heron shit and poplar leaves,
of water-soaked cottonwood trunks—
has been with you always,
ever since you stood in a riffle
with your father, casting
for steelhead, or earlier
as you sat in the warm shallows
of a backwater, your parents
picking berries behind you.

That's when you breathed and the scent
settled in the cells of your lungs
so even now it's a mystery
in your breath. And when you're close
to death it's what they'll smell
when they bend to kiss you.

Notes

Dedication to Quinton Duval: These lines are from Quinton's poem "The Wind from the South" in his early book *Dinner Music* (Lost Roads Press, 1984).

Epigraph: The Gerard Manley Hopkins epigraph is from his poem "Spring."

"Twig by Twig": The title of this poem is a phrase from Archibald MacLeish's "Ars Poetica."

"Hit by Pitch": In baseball, custom holds that, when hit by a pitch, a batter will not rub the place the ball has struck him even though that is what he most wants to do to alleviate the pain.

"The Sea of Galilee and the Sacramento River": This poem references *Luke*, Chapter 5.

"Trash Fish": Zuckweiler's Department Store was part of the Cone and Kimball Building, built in Red Bluff, California in 1886 and destroyed by fire in 1984. It was topped by a prominent clocktower, a landmark visible from great distances.

"Dig": The child's skeleton was likely of Nomlaki or Yana ancestry, two tribes whose borders met along the Sacramento River in Northern California.

"The Weather and Your Dress": The Theodore Roethke epigraph is from his poem "I Knew a Woman."

"Wolf and Lamb": The epigraph is from *Isaiah* 11:6 of the *King James Bible*.

About the Author

Albert Garcia is the author of two previously published books of poems, *Rainshadow* (Copper Beech Press) and *Skunk Talk* (Bear Star Press). He has also published *Digging In: Literature for Developing Writers* (Prentice Hall). His individual poems have been published in *North American Review, Mid-American Review, Poetry East, Willow Springs, Southern Poetry Review, Yankee,* and many other journals while also being featured in Ted Kooser's *American Life in Poetry* and Garrison Keillor's *A Writer's Almanac.* Albert taught community college English for eighteen years, and for the last ten years has served as a dean at Sacramento City College. He lives with his wife and family in Wilton, California, a rural area outside of Sacramento, where he grows most varieties of fruit trees that thrive in the region and several that don't.

Our Mission

The mission of Brick Road Poetry Press is to publish and promote poetry that entertains, amuses, edifies, and surprises a wide audience of appreciative readers. We are not qualified to judge who deserves to be published, so we concentrate on publishing what we enjoy. Our preference is for poetry geared toward dramatizing the human experience in language rich with sensory image and metaphor, recognizing that poetry can be, at one and the same time, both familiar as the perspiration of daily labor and as outrageous as a carnival sideshow.

BRICK ROAD
POETRY PRESS

Also Available from Brick Road Poetry Press

www.brickroadpoetrypress.com

Etch and Blur by Jamie Thomas

Water-Rites by Ann E. Michael

Bad Behavior by Michael Steffen

Tracing the Lines by Susanna Lang

Rising to the Rim by Carol Tyx

Treading Water with God by Veronica Badowski

Rich Man's Son by Ron Self

Just Drive by Robert Cooperman

The Alp at the End of My Street by Gary Leising

The Word in Edgewise by Sean M. Conrey

Household Inventory by Connie Jordan Green

Practice by Richard M. Berlin

Also Available from Brick Road Poetry Press

www.brickroadpoetrypress.com

Dancing on the Rim by Clela Reed

Possible Crocodiles by Barry Marks

Pain Diary by Joseph D. Reich

Otherness by M. Ayodele Heath

Drunken Robins by David Oates

Damnatio Memoriae by Michael Meyerhofer

Lotus Buffet by Rupert Fike

The Melancholy MBA by Richard Donnelly

Two-Star General by Grey Held

Chosen by Toni Thomas

About the Prize

The Brick Road Poetry Prize, established in 2010, is awarded annually for the best book-length poetry manuscript. Entries are accepted August 1st through November 1st. The winner receives $1000 and publication. For details on our preferences and the complete submission guidelines, please visit our website at www.brickroadpoetrypress.com.